Train Y
Iguana

Think Past the Emotional Barriers to Success in Family Law

By Preston Park, J.D.
Law Office of Preston Park, PLLC
Plano, Texas

https://planocustodyhelp.com
Tel: 972-454-9743

Additional copies are available at special quantity discounts for bulk purchases for sales promotions, premiums, fundraising, and educational use. For more information, please contact:
Law Offices of Preston Park, PLLC
Telephone: 972-454-9743

Brief Contents

Table of Contents

Introduction
Why I wrote this book

I have seen parents become emotionally and financially ruined by repeated returns to court to defend child custody cases. Through years of practicing law, hundreds of Legal Aid interviews, and my own personal growth, I recognize that hurt feelings, distrust, and fear of what is going to happen create emotional blinders that make us see things and react in ways that are unhelpful to our children and us. That is why I believe we need to repair our mindsets first to find a path to a better future – through professional counseling if possible – before finalizing a divorce or child custody case.

In short, my firm believes in thinking past the emotional barriers to make smart decisions in divorce and child custody cases to end the cycle of kicking child custody issues down the road.

How to read this book

I am not a neuroscientist or psychologist. I've merely done a lot of reading, personal growth, and observation and I believe that I have some useful ideas to offer people going through difficult custody and divorce cases.

Think of this book as grandpa sitting at the dinner table sharing stories and telling you what he thinks about life. I hope you find some of the ideas in this book useful to reflect on, but this book is not an authoritative textbook on the subject of human or iguana behavior.

Phoebe and Carl – a mostly made-up example

Phoebe and Carl divorced five years ago and have a ten-year-old son, Carl Jr. Phoebe and Carl remained committed to cooperating in raising their son until Phoebe moved in with her new boyfriend, Michael. Michael and Carl belong to different political parties.

Michael has strong political opinions and believes Carl's party's beliefs are immoral. Michael goes out of his way to be kind and fair to Phoebe and Carl Jr. but does not hide his disdain for Carl. Michael blames Carl and his political beliefs for the breakup of Carl and Phoebe's marriage which was very hard on Carl Jr. Michael even blames Carl for his own relationship problems with Phoebe and his inability to find a job.

Although Carl Jr. loved his father, because of the toxic attitude about him at his mother's house, he felt uncomfortable expressing anything positive about him. Michael always handled the exchanges, and when Michael asked Carl Jr. if he had fun with his father, Carl Jr. always responded, "No." Over time, the exchanges became increasingly stressful for Carl Jr.

Because of the stress Carl Jr. was showing at exchange time, Phoebe and Michael believed that Carl must be doing something horrible to cause it. On Michael's insistence, Phoebe sued Carl for changes to the custody order. Unfortunately, Carl was over-paying child support and had very little money available to fight, but he asked for mediation.

At mediation, Phoebe and Michael insisted that Carl see a therapist to correct his bad behavior. Carl found this offensive but his love and desire to see his son were greater than the emotional barriers created by his ego and need to be right. The parties agreed for Carl and Carl Jr. to have therapy to correct "Carl's bad behavior."

A week later Carl and Carl Jr. visited with the therapist separately. The therapist quickly diagnosed the problem and created a treatment plan to teach Carl Jr. how to think past the emotional barriers between him and his father that Michael had helped to create. Even though Phoebe and Michael were never able to get past their emotional barriers and continued to blame Carl and his politics, Carl Jr. was able to go back to making amazing memories with his father and maintain his relationship with both parents.

It's unfortunate that ego and the need to be right often result in legal battles that are costly both financially and to the mental and physical health of the children when they could be prevented with some family counseling. That's why our firm's goal is to help parents find solutions, not just file lawsuits.

Chapter 1

How is a divorce like an iguana fight?

The iguana is the rudder that steers the big ship.

In the Triune Brain Model, the human brain is divided into the reptilian brain (survival), limbic system (emotions), and neocortex (higher thinking). Or, as I like to think of it, your iguana brain, your horse brain, and your big brain. In most places, I will shorten that even further and refer to them as you, your horse, and your iguana. I'm not a neuroscientist or a psychologist, so this isn't meant to be a scientific treatise but rather a philosophical way to look at the world that I hope you will find useful.

Let's start with our big brain, "you." That's the brain which we think of as being who we are. We also tend to think

6

that this is the part of the brain we are using whether we are or not. We tend to believe that people we are emotionally disagreeing with are using the lower parts of the brain while we are being logical and intellectual.

A good way to think of the big brain is as the part of the brain you are trying to get your children to use when you say, "Use your words." It isn't easy to do that as we think it is. Even if they are chasing each other with sticks shouting insults, children will still make excuses that there is some justification. They think they are using their big brains when it's clear to everyone else that they are not.

We don't like to use our big brains as much as we think we do. Our big brain takes a lot of energy. I can't spend more than a couple of hours at a time working on this book before I am ready for a break. Using our big brains drains us. Chasing people with sticks is invigorating.

Horses just want to have fun, but they can be trained to work.

Next, our "horse" brain is the one we spend most of our time training and the one we prefer to use. We teach it how to ride a bike, how to swim, how to drive a car, and how to find the way home. We can drive to the park and chat away merrily using our big brains while our horse brains take us where we are going. Sometimes we find ourselves in the driveway when we meant to stop at the grocery store because our big brains wandered off and let our horses take us home.

Good businesses have policies and procedures in part because they make us more efficient by training our horse brains how to execute a process instead of thinking through it each time. Good businesses also offer rewards to help motivate us to work harder.

Iguanas just want to be safe, but they can be trained to let people hold them.

Finally, we have our "iguana" brains. The iguana is mostly instinct. It wants to eat, reproduce, stay alive, and protect its territory. You'll notice that as we go further down, our brains get dumber but more powerful. The iguana is the rudder that steers the big ship if you are willing to take the metaphors even deeper.

An advertisement with a pretty model next to the fancy car tells your iguana that you need that fancy car so you can reproduce. Your iguana tells your horse to go buy it, your horse decides to take out a loan, and your big brain thinks "you" thought of the whole thing. Nobody thinks they bought a car and went into debt because they saw advertisements, yet advertising works well enough for companies to spend a lot of money on them.

Your big brain may want you on a diet, but your horse brain wants to eat those cookies in the oven. Your horse may want to eat those cookies, but your iguana isn't going to let you touch them until they've cooled down for a few minutes – that is, unless you've trained your horse and iguana not to eat cookies at all, but that's a topic for a different book.

It is a little more complicated than that because you, your horse, and your iguana all have access to the same memories. You have three brains but one mind. They are all you.

The horse and iguana influence our decisions without explaining why (iguanas don't speak English), so we end up making reasons up. You decide intellectually that you want to lose weight, but the horse wants cookies. The horse wants cookies, so you make up a story that the cookies are a reward for exercising even though you will still lose ground in your diet after the exercise. Maybe you never even get around to exercising because your horse found a TV show it thinks you need to watch.

People who were bullied or abused often have quiet voices, like someone turned their volume way down. Their iguanas are afraid to be loud because that will attract predators so they will find all sorts of ways to resist speaking up. "That's just how I am. I'm just a quiet person."

Your horse doesn't want to go to a job interview because you are insecure and were criticized at the last one, so you make up an excuse that the job is not a good fit for you. It's not that you're deliberately lying to yourself, but the stories are being made up from all of the information and memories in your head somewhere between you and your iguana.

Your iguana doesn't want you to have a friendly divorce.

People often think they can have an amicable divorce, but as soon as they start talking property division and child support, their iguanas wake up and get ready to defend their territory. Then they start making up stories in their heads:

- *She just wants to destroy me.*
- *She wants to take everything I have.*
- *She doesn't care about our child; she just wants child support.*
- *He wants me to have nothing and end up on the street.*
- *He's throwing me away like a piece of garbage.*
- *He doesn't care about our child; he just doesn't want to pay child support.*

Sometimes the bad things are true, but most of my clients seem to be decent people who are just trying to put food on their table and move on with their lives.

How do I get my iguana under control if I know my ex is evil and I'm not just making up stories?

With or without making up stories, my ex is an evil person. How will training my iguana help?

The sad truth that I can't spare you from is that there are really horrible people in the world who never face the consequences of their actions. There are rapists, murderers, kidnappers, and even slavers walking free who continue to get away with their crimes. And it's not that no one knows who they are. Some people are just hard to catch and even harder to convict. Witnesses disappear, are killed, are too scared to testify, or lie in court due to extortion, bribery, or even loyalty.

Your ex may or may not be that bad – and I have seen some that are that bad – but if the law can't get them with all of its resources, a family lawyer in a civil courtroom may not be able to do any better. That's the reality we are stuck with.

The question you have to ask yourself is, do you want to face that reality using your big brain or your iguana brain? I've seen a lot of brilliant people make dumb decisions because they let their iguana brains take over. People with advanced degrees, even doctorates, will fail to show up in court, make a scene in church, go after their abusive ex with a baseball bat, and do all sorts of things that make themselves look awful and make their lives even worse to the delight of their tormentors. Imagine an iguana seeing the shadow of a pigeon, running onto the freeway to escape, and getting hit by a truck. That's not the path to a better future.

No matter how bad things are, we have no trouble making them worse for ourselves when we don't think. It may be that you can't make the judge see how evil your ex is, but you can be smart and at least avoid letting your iguana run onto the freeway. There may even be a nice, safe, warm rock to shelter by if you take time to look. See the Gray Rock method in Chapter 5.

Chapter 2

How do I get started training my iguana?

Self-help

Your iguana can be trained to help you, or at least not get in your way, just like your horse can. The hard way is doing it yourself. There are a lot of self-help books out there to get you started if you search under "personal growth." Books that might come in handy include *How to Lose at Everything and Still Win Big* by Scott Adams; *Think and Grow Rich* by Napoleon Hill; and *The 15 Invaluable Laws of Growth: Live Them and Reach Your Potential* by John Maxwell, to name a few.

A common theme among self-improvement programs is the idea of auto-suggestion. Auto-suggestion is some ritual you perform to "trick your subconscious" into figuring out how to reach your goals. I accidentally discovered this process independently when studying for multiple choice tests. I found that if I took the test as fast as I could then immediately retook it before turning it in, my brain kept working behind the scenes and had the right answer to replace my "best guess" the second time around. When you make a target for your brain to hit, it will work behind the scenes to help you make it happen.

The first step is to define the goal:

1. Write down what you think the goal is.
2. Ask yourself why you have that goal.
3. Ask yourself why that answer matters to you.
4. Ask yourself why the previous answer is important to you.

The answer to number four is usually the answer. It might be number three or two, but it's probably not number one unless you've thoroughly thought things through already.

For example:

1. I want custody of our child. *Why?*
2. I want custody because the other parent is letting him slack off at school. *Why is that important?*
3. If our child slacks off at school, he won't reach his full potential. *Why does that matter to me?*
4. If our child doesn't reach his full potential, he won't achieve the dream he shared with us before the divorce of being a marine biologist, and I'll always blame myself.

Number four is your goal:

Our child is going to reach his full potential and become a marine biologist so that I can feel good as a parent knowing that my child achieved his dreams.

People can argue whether that is a healthy goal for you to have or not, but it's up to you to find the right one.

The last step is to write down your goal seven times every night before you go to bed and when you wake up in the morning. That's it. Let your iguana take it from there.

It might be that you end up with an answer other than filing a lawsuit and getting custody of your child. That's why you want to focus on the goal at the bottom of the list. Your iguana isn't going to let you come up with the right answer otherwise.

As an attorney, it is hard to tell people that it doesn't sound like they need a divorce, or they don't need a modification based on what they told me. Not only because that's how I make my money, but also because their iguanas came in ready for a fight. They don't want to consider the possibility of a better way, and their iguanas may want to fight me over it.

Get help

Think about why you want to go the self-help route. Is that really the right thing to do, or is that your iguana getting you to make up stories about why you shouldn't ask for help? A lot of people have huge emotional barriers against finding professional help. They think it would mean they are weak or crazy or incompetent. They've heard jokes or seen comedies about hopeless people talking to their exasperated therapists. Their iguanas see those memories and put up a big fight to keep their humans from appearing weak and looking like prey to the predators of the world.

Think of counseling, coaching, co-parenting programs, or therapy as taking your iguana to obedience school. It doesn't mean you can't do it yourself. It means that you are smart enough to go to a professional to coach you through training your iguana versus doing it yourself and wasting time. Surely you can think of better uses for that time you would save, can't you? That doesn't mean don't read books; they are still full of useful information but don't hire yourself to train your iguana when there are so many professionals who can help you do it better and faster.

The Dale Carnegie Course is an excellent iguana training course that I can recommend to anyone whether they are going through a court fight or not. It's nine weeks of training your iguana to speak up and be more self-confident. It is a little expensive, and somewhat of a commitment, but your iguana will thank you for it.

Why did you start with self-help if getting help is so much better?

Why start with self-help if get-help is the better option? Because self-help will probably lead you to get-help anyway. I started focusing my iguana on becoming a better lawyer a few years ago. I spent about two years reading and researching how persuasion works and how we think before stumbling across the Dale Carnegie Course and other programs that I have been involved in. Because of the studying, I understood why these types of programs work, so it was easy to make the jump. Feel free to skip past the two years of research and head straight into get-help though.

Get Collaborative Law

Collaborative law professionals are the iguana wranglers of divorce. They are trained to help the parties think past their emotions and find creative solutions to divorce issues.

Collaborative law is a cooperative path in which the parties work together outside the courtroom and make their own decisions with the guidance of their lawyers and often additional professionals. The team usually consists of at least an attorney for each party, a mental health professional, and a financial advisor. It could also include a child specialist, career counselor, and other professionals or experts who participate as needed.

Even though it is collaborative, the collaborative law process does not require the parties to like each other or even be able to get along. They can continue to hate each other while the professionals keep the parties working towards finding a solution that protects each party's own interests. However, the collaborative law process is completely voluntary, so either party can terminate it at any time. The collaborative process also terminates when either side elects to request court intervention.

The team

Attorneys. The attorneys in a collaborative law case keep their clients informed about the status of their case; comply with their clients' reasonable requests for information; explain things to the client to the extent reasonably necessary to permit their clients to make informed decisions; assist their clients in setting realistic goals; and advocate for their client's interests. They also have additional duties such as to inquire into any history of family violence and terminate the process if it has occurred and cannot be reasonably addressed.

Neutral Mental Health Professional. The mental health professional facilitates communication between the parties. Their job is to help the parties overcome their emotions and focus, on their objectives, and think to find creative solutions.

Neutral Financial Expert. The financial expert assists the parties in collecting financial information about the estate. They can assist in combining inventories, determining the appropriate value of personal and real property, and calculating incomes. They can also help the parties make decisions about how to divide the property.

Neutral Child Specialist. The child specialist meets with the children and parents, facilitates the development of a parenting plan, and facilitates communication between the children and parents. The child specialist may also advise parents as to additional professional support for the children.

Other Advisors. Other advisors such as real estate agents, financial planners, insurance agents, and appraisers can be brought in as necessary.

Isn't a good compromise one where everyone leaves angry?

Everyone doesn't have to leave angry to make a good compromise. Consider the commonly-cited "orange" example: Ralph and Dianne each want the orange. How do you decide who gets it?

Trial: Ralph and Dianne put on evidence to convince a judge that he or she deserves the orange. Ralph says he bought it. Dianne says she does all of the cooking. They argue back and forth until the judge gets tired of listening to them and orders the orange to be cut in half. Result: Both Ralph and Dianne leave angry.

Collaborative Law: Ralph and Dianne meet with the team to discuss their goals. Ralph explains that he wants to make orange tea. He needs all of the rind to mix in with his other ingredients in order to make enough tea. Dianne explains that she wants to make orange muffins. She needs all of the juice for her orange muffin recipe. The collaborative expert analyzes the problem and describes a method to extract all of the juice from the orange while leaving the rind for Ralph. Result: Tea and muffins.

The above is based on the "Parable of the Orange" from the "Collaborative Divorce Texas" site noted in the resources section. The parable has been passed around for a while, and I don't know the original source.

Why doesn't everyone use collaborative law?

Collaborative law isn't for everyone. If one of the parties is dishonest and completely untrustworthy, or if there is a history of violence or abuse, it's not going to be possible to overcome those barriers to collaboration. There is usually no formal discovery, but each party must agree and be committed to full and candid disclosure of all information requested unless limited by agreement. The level of openness required is a big challenge for some people, but the experts can usually help overcome that.

Generally, collaborative law costs the same or less than litigation. The parties are doing most of the heavy lifting themselves under the direction of the experts and advisors. Although the parties are expected to cooperate in disclosure, collaborative law is a confidential process externally. That means the experts and advisors used will not be testifying in court if the collaborative process does not result in an agreement. Even the attorneys will have to be replaced if the parties decide to go to trial.

Pro tip: In some Texas courts, it is possible to electronically file everything and finalize your divorce by affidavit without anyone ever going anywhere near the courthouse.

Even if Collaborative Law isn't an option, having the advice of the same types of experts can help keep your own mind under control.

Get educated

One way to get some confidence and help your iguana along is by gaining some knowledge. You can do some research online or go to the TexasLawHelp.org site to read up on Family Law issues. Familiar things are less scary for your iguana so you will be able to think more clearly. Following this chapter, I've included answers to some common questions or issues that come up in divorce and child custody cases.

Chapter 3

What do I need to know about getting a divorce in Texas?

What are the ten steps of a divorce in Texas?

1. The Decision. First, you must decide whether you need a divorce. This isn't always as easy as it sounds. You think that a divorce will solve some problem that you have. If your spouse is abusive or cheating on you, then divorce is likely to be the better option in dealing with it. But if the problems are financial, emotional, or something else, you may have better ways to solve your problem. Even if you think you have "tried everything," chances are you haven't tried anything half as emotionally and financially draining as a divorce.

2. Preparation. How are you going to survive for the first seven years after your divorce? You may not have thought that far ahead. Do you have a budget and a plan for how you are going to meet your needs post-divorce? How are you going to pay child support, rent, insurance, and all the other expenses in a divided household? Do you want to try Collaborative Law? Who are you going to hire to be your attorney? How are you going to pay attorney fees? Where will you live while the divorce is pending?

3. The Petition. The first legal step in a divorce is filing the Original Petition for Divorce and paying the filing fee. The petition states the grounds for the divorce and the relief that the petitioner is requesting from the court.

4. Service of Citation. After the petition is filed, it along with a citation must be served on the respondent. The citation is a document prepared by the clerk under the seal of the court that has information that the respondent needs to know in order to respond to the divorce suit. The citation and petition must be served on the respondent by a sheriff, constable, or licensed process server. The respondent can sign a waiver of service of the citation to avoid this expense.

5. The Answer. The respondent has until the Monday following twenty days of receipt of citation to file an answer. The answer can contain a general denial, denials of specific allegations, and counterclaims. A typical answer contains a general denial and a request for attorney fees.

6. The Counter-petition. Counter-petitions are optional. A counter-petition is a petition filed by the respondent of the original petition. Counter-petitions are filed when the respondent has claims to make against the petitioner. They can also be filed to keep the suit alive in case the petitioner dismisses his own case.

7. Temporary Orders. Temporary orders are also optional. Parties request them to preserve assets while the divorce is pending, or to make orders regarding the children until the divorce is final. They may include a temporary restraining order or temporary injunction to make sure the parties behave themselves during the divorce process and may include an order to mediate. Temporary orders can be agreed, or a judge can decide on temporary orders after a hearing.

8. Discovery. The discovery process is where the parties exchange information necessary to determine what will go into the final order. Discovery can start as soon as the divorce is filed and can be informal or formal. Informal discovery consists of requests between the parties or between their attorneys for information that they think they will need to finalize the divorce. It is usually cheaper than formal discovery. In formal discovery, the parties serve each other requests to produce documents, disclose certain information about the lawsuit, answer interrogatories, answer depositions, and make admissions or denials. Third parties can also be subpoenaed and deposed during the discovery process.

9. The Final Trial. Almost every divorce ends in a final trial. If the divorce is agreed, only the petitioner typically shows up for the trial, gives evidence, and asks the judge to sign the order. Some courts allow the petitioner to file an affidavit with the final order so that no one must go to court and there is no trial. If the parties can't agree on the terms for the final order, then either the judge or a jury will decide after a contested hearing.

10. Motion to Enter. Unfortunately, even after the final trial is held and the judge or jury rules, sometimes parties still can't agree on language for the final order. When that happens, the parties must appear before the judge at least one more time to have the judge rule on the language and sign the order.

On what grounds can I get a divorce in Texas?

In Texas, there are both fault grounds and no-fault grounds for divorce. You can get a divorce in Texas just because you don't get along and you don't want to be married anymore. You can also get a no-fault divorce because you have been living apart for three years or because your spouse has been confined to a mental institution for three years.

Fault grounds include adultery, cruelty, conviction of a felony, or abandonment for over a year. Adultery, conviction, and abandonment are self-explanatory. Cruelty is when one spouse's behavior or actions are so bad that they destroyed the ability of the couple to continue to live together as husband and wife.

Fault grounds are a factor in determining how the property should be divided and whether one spouse should get a larger share of the estate.

Cruelty Examples

Martha and Jacob

Jacob started going to the gym and lost 40 pounds. People began complementing Jacob on his new looks. This made Martha insecure and jealous. Martha started criticizing Jacob for his new body, the new clothes he had to buy, and for making new friends who shared his new lifestyle. Martha's criticisms gradually escalated, and she started calling him ever nastier names and accusing him of cheating on her. Jacob had to face Martha's worsening criticisms and accusations every single time he came home for nearly _two years_. He finally realized that he could no longer live like this and filed for divorce.

Jacob strenuously denied any infidelity and Martha offered no evidence that he had been unfaithful. A judge found cruelty grounds and gave Jacob a larger share of the community property.

Julie and Bart

Julie worked at a bank for 26 years. Her annual salary was $50,000 per year. Before Julie filed for divorce, Bart gave Julie permission to withdraw $50 from his checking account containing community funds. Bart was the only signatory for the account. After Julie withdrew the funds with her signature, Bart reported her to the bank. The bank investigated and fired Julie for violating its code of ethics.

The trial court found that Bart's conduct was cruel treatment and awarded Julie a money judgment.

How is it fair that my spouse gets to take half my business in the divorce when I put in all the work, and she had almost nothing to do with it?

Divorce and custody cases are iguana fights. How is it fair that my spouse gets to take half my business in the divorce when I put in all the work, and she had almost nothing to do with it? People's iguanas are very territorial about their stuff. That goes especially for property division and for child support.

Let's see what happens when we take the emotion out of it.

Bill has a great idea for a business, but he doesn't have any money. Amy likes his idea and offers him $1000 to be a silent partner who owns half the company. Bill accepts. Bill's business takes off, and twenty-five years later he sells his business for $10 million. Amy owns half the business, so she takes her $5 million share since that is what she bargained for and there are no complaints from Bill. There is no controversy because it's just business.

Let's see what happens when we put the emotion back into it from Amy's perspective. Bill is in love with Amy. Amy likes Bill but is not all that interested. Bill is persistent. He tells Amy they are perfect for each other, that he's going places, he'll make her life wonderful and she should marry him instead of any of the other boys who want her. Even though he is poor, they are young and in love, and he eventually gets her to marry him.

Soon they have two children. Amy stays home and takes care of their two kids while Bill works hard for twenty-five years, slowly climbing the corporate ladder until he becomes an executive in a hardware business. The children grow up, and Bill has a new sense of freedom.

Bill decides to leave his wife for his beautiful young secretary. Meanwhile, Amy hasn't had a job in twenty-five years, has few job skills, can never have children again, and does not look as young as she used to look. Bill thinks,

"The house, retirement accounts, and all of that property are mine because I worked hard all of my life for it while my lazy wife stayed home with the kids all day."

The fact is Amy invested in Bill's life when she married him. She invested a heck of a lot more than the Amy that gave Bill $1000 to start a business. The state of Texas sees it that way too, and that's why she has a right to her share of the community estate.

Bill's iguana is fighting for territory while Amy's iguana is fighting for the safety and security she is losing. Bill has the advantage. Bill's iguana knows that Amy's iguana is worried about survival. Bill's iguana can make threats to scare Amy's iguana into accepting low offers or risk ending up without enough to survive.

Because of that, Amy will start making up stories in her head about how she doesn't want a big ugly divorce, and she just wants the marriage to be over so she will take Bill's first offer for the security in knowing what she will get. That's how Amy's iguana can be defeated by Bill's iguana if she doesn't get it under control.

Chapter 4

What do I need to know about child custody in Texas?

What is a Parenting Plan?

A parenting plan is a plan for how separated parents are going to cooperate in raising their children. It includes conservatorship to determine who is going to make certain decisions regarding the child's health, welfare, and education, or how the parents are going to cooperate in making those decisions. It also includes a visitation schedule to determine who has the children when and where the children are exchanged.

In Texas, visitation is typically either the standard possession schedule or the extended standard possession schedule.

In the standard possession order, the parent without the right to designate the primary residence of the children or possessory conservator has possession of the children during the school year on the first, third, and fifth Friday of the month for the weekend; and on Thursday evenings from 6:00 pm to 8:00 pm. Summers and holidays are treated differently with the parents having a different holiday schedule depending on whether it is an even or odd year.

In the extended standard possession order, the possessory conservator has the children every Thursday from the time they leave school on Thursday until school starts on Friday morning. On the first, third, and fifth during the school year, the possessory conservator has the children from the time they leave school on Thursday until they return to school on Monday morning, except while they are in school on Friday.

What is conservatorship?

In Texas, courts presume that both parents are going to be able to cooperate in raising their children.

Joint managing conservatorship

In Texas, parents are presumed to be able to cooperate in raising their children, even when they're separated, and that is what is called joint managing conservatorship. Joint managing conservatorship means that the parents are going to share certain decision-making responsibilities when it comes to the kids' health and education.

Even if the parents have joint managing conservatorship, some decisions can be made exclusive to one parent only.

Garth and Tami are getting a divorce. Garth has been abusive in the past, but in the preceding two years he is only verbally abusive – continually belittling Tami, her friends, and her family in front of their young children and preventing her from seeing family or getting a job, without actually getting physical.

Tami would rather not go to court, and the two parents cannot afford expert evaluations and testimony, but Garth is a pro at manipulation and Tami is afraid that Garth will manipulate the children against her over time. Tami settles for joint managing conservatorship but keeps the exclusive right to make mental health and educational decisions for the children. After the divorce, Tami can get counseling for her children to help deal with Garth's constant negativity without having to ask for Garth's permission.

Your iguana might be saying, "That's terrible that Tami is stuck with the expense and hassle of keeping the kids in counseling to deal with Garth's bad behavior!" However, with today's connected world, manipulation and parental alienation can be inflicted across many miles and oceans. It may not be long before it's even done from space.

Keeping it out in the open and inoculating the children from its effects may turn out to be a blessing for them.

Sole managing conservatorship

Sometimes divorced parents simply can't agree on how to raise their children. Other times the legislature has determined that parents should not have to agree on how to raise their children.

When there's sole managing conservatorship, it means the court has found some reason why the parents can't cooperate and gives most or some major decision-making abilities to only one parent instead of both.

By default, the sole managing conservator has the exclusive right to consent to invasive or mental health treatment for the children, designate the children's primary residence, receive child support, and make educational decisions. The possessory conservator (other parent) can be informed about the children's medical, mental, and educational situation; make decisions in an emergency; and confer with school officials among other things.

Some of the sole managing conservator's exclusive rights can be made joint or independent. This is useful for situations where one parent has to be sole managing conservator by law, but it is in the children's best interest for the parents to share some decision-making responsibilities.

Why do evil stepmothers exist?

All sorts of stories get made up in custody cases. Imagine there is a camera recording everything you do in life. If at the end of your life, it is edited to remove everything good you ever did and only the worst things remain – or even good things that look bad out of context, then you would look like a horrible person.

The Tale of: "A Boy and His Best Friend" or "The Psychopathic Horse-Killer"

Our emotions color the way we see the world, and even what we perceive. Our brains have something like a movie soundtrack playing all the time and sometimes do some creative editing to match reality to our feelings. Just the title is enough to steer how you feel about the pictures playing on the screen.

Wyatt had a beautiful gray mare named Gracie. She was a gift from Wyatt's father when she was just a colt. Gracie was Wyatt's responsibility. He had to feed her, clean her, make sure her stall was clean, even train her. Two different directors make movies about Wyatt and Gracie. One makes "A Boy and His Best Friend," and the other makes "The Psychopathic Horse-Killer." Let' see how they turn out.

A Boy and His Best Friend

"A Boy and His Best Friend" opens with a bright, cheerful melody as young Wyatt's father presents him with Gracie. The boy grins from ear to ear and nods as his father explains to him that Gracie is his mare and she can't raise herself, so her life is his responsibility.

The music is brave and determined as Wyatt and Gracie grow up together. Come rain or shine Wyatt sometimes marches, sometimes runs, and sometimes drags himself out to the barn to take care of her. His father coaches him through breaking her. Wyatt works her consistently over the weeks months and years. The music crescendos in fanfare as he gallops over a hill and stops by a little creek in the valley to rest.

Suddenly, the worst happens. Out of nowhere Gracie is bitten by a snake and has a severe, crippling and fatal reaction.

Wyatt's father explains to him that Gracie can't be helped. She is his responsibility, and all he can do is end her suffering. "Don't think. Just march right up to her and shoot her between the eyes. Then you can grieve, not before." Wyatt does what he was told. He marches up to Gracie, shoots her between the eyes, and then collapses in grief.

The Psychopathic Horse-Killer

The next director has a different interpretation of what the story means. He creates a film called, "The Psychopathic Horse-Killer." It opens with a dark, foreboding theme as young Wyatt's father presents him with Gracie. The boy grins from ear to ear and nods as his father explains to him that Gracie is his mare and she can't raise herself, so her life is his responsibility. The music is ominous. It's obvious from the title how this movie ends, whom the villain is, and whom the victim will be.

The music is angry and hateful as Wyatt sometimes marches, and sometimes drags himself out to the barn to take care of Gracie and as his father coaches him through breaking her. Wyatt works her unendingly over the weeks months and years. The music crescendos in misery as he gallops over a hill and slowly approaches the little creek in the shadow of the valley. Demonic melodies fill the theater as Wyatt marches up to poor Gracie and the screen goes dark as the shot rings out.

With a little bit of creative editing and the right soundtrack, you can make completely different stories out of the same facts. We do the same thing in our own heads. If you knew Wyatt personally, the movie you made in your head out of his story would depend on whether you love him or hate him.

In the same way, when our loved ones pass away, all of the bad things are forgotten, edited out of their movie, and all that is left in our hearts is love. That is the soundtrack through which we recall their lives. When we divorce, the soundtrack goes sour. Suddenly, nothing she ever did was good or sincere. She became a monster.

Carl and Phoebe Revisited

If you didn't read the introduction, go back and read it now. In the example of Carl and Phoebe in the Introduction, Carl Jr.'s mother and step-father believed that Carl Jr. didn't want to see Carl anymore.

They couldn't see that it was the toxic environment they were creating that was making Carl Jr. confused. It wasn't because they are evil. Remember, we're only seeing edited versions of their lives too. Their problem was that their iguanas were getting them to make up stories about Carl, so they were unable to see the distress they were causing Carl Jr.'s iguana, even though it was pretty obvious to anyone else.

They had the wrong soundtracks. Carl prevailed because he didn't let his iguana get in the way with stories about all the reasons he shouldn't agree to therapy.

Chapter 5

How can I win my child custody case in Texas?

What does it mean to you to "win" child custody? Why is it important to you? What would happen if you didn't win during the divorce? What does your life look after your divorce if you win? What does it look like for your kids? What if you won after the divorce?

What I find generally is that parents are concerned about spending enough time with their kids after divorce, having a good relationship with their kids, their kids being raised correctly, not being shut out of important decisions and events in the children's lives, and not going broke paying child support. The best way to accomplish your goals is almost always through mediation, but only if someone has helped you think through the above questions and what you want to accomplish.

In mediation, both sides can often win because the conflict in values and personalities that led to the divorce in the first place lead to different goals. Often one side "wins" only in ways that don't matter because the attorney didn't take the time to truly understand his client and what matters to him.

What factors help determine the best interest for my children?

The court is going to look at anything that's relevant to the best interests of the child. But, among one of the most important factors, are the physical and emotional needs of the child, the stability of the home, how well the parents are able to cooperate, how close a parent lives to relatives or friends that are important to the child, the skills of the parents, who has been the primary caregiver up to this point, or things like if there's been any abuse or false accusations of abuse.

Do I forgo custody if I miss too many visitations?

No. You don't forgo custody for merely missing visitations. What you need to do is be a good and involved parent. Are you attending parent-teacher conferences? How involved are you in the children's extracurricular activities? Do you call regularly? Have you sent birthday and Christmas cards to your children every year? Are you caught up with child support?

It's never too late to start getting involved but be sure to do it the right way. Explain to your children – and to your ex if you are reasonably able to communicate – that you have decided to be a better parent. Ask who would be a good person to talk to at school and go talk to him. Find out about doctors' appointments. Start attending extracurricular activities and offer to help pay for them.

But be careful and try not to be disruptive when reinserting yourself into your children's routine. Do it gradually and communicate, but don't take no for an answer. When a parent is absent or uninvolved, it gives the impression that you don't care. If you suddenly start showing up to activities or asking about school, it is natural for your ex and your children to be suspicious of your motives. People are more likely to suspect you have ill motives than to believe you've suddenly decided to become a better parent, so be respectful of their feelings and take responsibility for your own part in contributing to them.

Courts want what is in the best interest of children. They want children to have a relationship with and as much contact as possible with both parents. It's not that unusual when absent parents suddenly realize they want to be a part of their children's lives. Judges welcome that. Just do it right and do it soon.

How Do I Get the Judge to See My Ex as a Narcissist?

Why does it matter to you for the judge to see your ex as a narcissist? What do you think the judge will do if he sees your ex as a narcissist? What do you want him to do? What impact will it have on your children if the judge sees your ex as a narcissist? How will it impact your goals for your children? What are your goals for your children?

The judge is never going to feel the way you do about your ex, and likely doesn't care whether your ex is a narcissist or not. The judge is interested in rendering orders that are in the best interest of the children.

Hurt feelings, distrust, and fear of what is going to happen create emotional blinders that make us see things and react in ways that are unhelpful our children and us. That is why we need to repair our mindsets first so that we can see a path to a better future before finalizing a divorce or child custody case.

The problem is, we see what we see, and our perceptions are our perceptions. We can't tell when our emotions are getting in the way of what we need to see. That is why even lawyers hire lawyers to help with their own cases. The fact that you need the judge to see the way you see is a hint that the emotional part of your brain might be interfering with the thinking part.

The right questions to ask are: "What parenting plan would give my children the best possible future," and "How can I help the judge decide this is the best parenting plan?" I highly recommend that you find a licensed professional counselor who can help you think past the emotional barriers created by the conflict with your ex so that you can better identify and articulate a plan to achieve your goals.

The best way to deal with the narcissist is to *not feed the trolls*.

How do I not feed the trolls?

Gray Rock Method

The Gray Rock Method was popularized a few years ago by a blogger named Skylar. The Gray Rock Method involves becoming boring. Your ex wants to see a reaction from your iguana – usually one that is detrimental to you and your case. Your ex is like a kid banging on the glass of a zoo enclosure trying to get a rise out of the animals. Once he sees a reaction that entertains him, he will gleefully exploit it and try to get even more.

If you can get your iguana to lay quietly and not respond to your ex's antics, then eventually your ex will move on. Keep in mind, he will keep returning to your enclosure at the worst times to try different things to get your iguana to attack and entertain him, so it is important that you keep it well trained.

Practice by reading emails or text messages from your ex. When one starts to make you upset, just notice that you are upset and move on without reacting. While you are at it, create a catalog or timeline of your ex's lies as that will come in handy in litigation.

BIFF Response® Method

BIFF stands for Brief Informative Friendly Firm and is a trademark of the High Conflict Institute. The number one rule BIFF and Gray Rock is, *Don't talk about BIFF and Gray Rock*. One thing high conflict people are good at is getting people to give away too much information. If you start giving up confidential information because your ex is saying things that aren't true or you don't like, then you are giving him ammunition to use against you later.

A BIFF Response® is one that:

1. Does not apologize. The not apologizing part is a key component BIFF to avoid feeding

your troll ex. It doesn't fit cleanly into the acronym, so just think "BIFF isn't sorry" to remember not to apologize in your responses.

2. Is Brief. Before you say or write anything, take a breath and organize your thoughts into the shortest answer possible.

3. Is Informative, but not overly informative. You don't need to justify yourself. If you are running late because you forgot to turn on the dryer, you only need to convey what time you will arrive, not your current dryer settings or what you just washed.

4. Is Friendly. This is the Gray Rock component. Don't give any excuse for drama. Suck it up and be nice, then give your iguana a nice pat on the head.

5. Is Firm. Don't be wishy-washy. You don't have to apologize or be self-conscious about your position. If your child needs to be at the dentist at 7:30, then say, "he needs

to be at the dentist at 7:30," not, "is there any way you can get him to the dentist by 7:30?"

Remember, your ex wants your iguana to try to bite, so give it a little reward for behaving. When you nail three out of the five BIFF components, think about how you can do better next time, but be happy with any improvement.

I would highly recommend getting some BIFF coaching. Your ex knows you well enough to be a pro at pushing your buttons. Outsmart him by getting help from your own pros. Sources for more information on BIFF and Gray Rock appear in the *Resources* section at the end of this book.

Chapter 6

Is Someone Going to Jail?

What types of court orders can be legally enforced?

Generally, an order can be enforced if it's an order signed by a judge. More specifically, an *enforceable* order can be enforced. An order is enforceable if it is specific, legal, and not against public policy.

<u>Specific</u>

Family Law orders are many dozens of pages long in part because the order has to be specific enough to be enforced. Every part of the order has to specifically tell who what to do where, when, and how. You can't have an order that just says, "Wash the dog every Sunday." What does washing mean? Is spraying it with a spray bottle enough? Letting him swim in the pool? The order has to say, "John is ordered to wash Rex, the dog, by scrubbing him with a brush in seven inches of lukewarm, soapy water in the Acme Dog Pool for six minutes, then rinse him thoroughly with clean, fresh water, every Sunday between 8:00 a.m. and 5:00 p.m." Otherwise, the court cannot determine whether John actually complied with the order.

Legal

An illegal order cannot be enforced. This seems obvious, but sometimes language gets into an order that the lawyers and judge did not know was illegal at the time. For example, Husband was wiretapping Wife in violation of federal and state laws. The final decree of divorce ordered Wife to return all records related to the wiretapping to Husband. Unfortunately, a criminal investigation of the wiretapping made it illegal for Wife to turn over the records because that would obstruct the investigation. The court could not enforce the order.

Not against public policy

Public policy will rarely come up. An example of something that might be against public policy and therefore unenforceable would be making child support contingent on visitation or visitation contingent on child support.

I was in a hearing recently, where we struggled in front of the Judge for quite some time to find language that would make dividing some international property legally enforceable. A lot of people have the misconception that, just because money is being ordered to be paid, that the order can't be enforced with jail time. That's not necessarily the case. Anytime you're involved in an enforcement, you should contact an attorney for advice.

Will my ex go to jail if he is found in contempt of our court order?

The purpose of an enforcement is to make sure your ex starts following orders and doesn't violate them again and cause you headaches. The judge may put your ex in jail if you ask, however, the judge can also suspend the sentence in exchange for your ex following the orders and additional orders that will prevent an enforcement in the future.

While the sentence is suspended, the person found guilty of contempt has to follow the rules specified during the suspension. If he violates the rules, then the judge can issue a warrant to have him arrested after a motion to revoke suspension is filed.

My ex is keeping my children from me to force me to pay child support. Is that legal?

It is illegal, but it might end up helping you. Most judges don't like to put both parents in jail for violating court orders. If the other parent starts violating court orders to try to force you to pay child support, that may be an opportunity for you to begin correcting your child support issues without the risk (or at least a lower risk) of going to jail. You should contact an attorney immediately to see about solving your child support problem and the visitation problem.

Can I go to jail for visiting my children too much?

Visiting your child too much is probably a violation of your order. It is another way of saying you have your child when the other parent has the right of possession.

A court ordered parenting plan is written to give children fair access to both parents. Either parent deciding that he should have more time with the children without the other's permission is deciding that the Court was wrong. Judge's don't like that. They also don't like it if you disrespect the Court by disobeying the Court's order. If one parent can prove beyond a reasonable doubt the other is visiting his children against orders without permission, a Judge can and often will put him in jail.

Can I go to jail because I missed some payments and it wasn't my fault?

As of June 14, 2013, you can no longer avoid jail simply by showing your child support is up to date at the enforcement hearing. In 2014 there was a news story about a man named Clifford who was jailed in just such a case. His original hearing was set for June 10, 2013, four days before the law that would allow him to avoid jail was repealed; however, it was reset by agreement to give the father time to make one more payment because, unfortunately, Clifford had erroneously believed he was up to date before the June 10 hearing. By the time of the new hearing, the repealed law could no longer help him avoid jail.

Clifford also tried to argue that the missing child support was the fault of his employer. He claimed that an employee incorrectly entered the withholding amounts from his paycheck. The problem with that argument is that you, not your employer, are responsible for ensuring child support is paid correctly. Your order even says this. You do not get to enjoy the benefits of your employer's mistakes at the expense of your children.

The Houston Court of Appeals did overturn one violation where the trial court found the father guilty of paying too much child support. Unfortunately for Clifford, the appeals court was able to overturn only this part of the order and leave the remaining violations and Clifford's jail sentence intact.

Chapter 7

What can I do to help my kids through this?

How can I protect my children from the negativity of divorce?

Divorce is always hard on kids, no matter how amicable you are with your ex-spouse. Emotions are running high on all sides, making it especially hard to be the perfect parent—but there are still steps you can take to soften the blow of divorce on your children. Here are a few ways to shelter your kids from the more negative aspects of divorce.

Have an age-appropriate conversation.

You'll eventually need to have "the talk" with your kids about the divorce, and it's best if you plan this ahead of time. If possible, you should explain the situation jointly with your (soon-to-be) ex-spouse. Make sure you explain it in a way that's appropriate for your child's age. A younger child might need a very simplified explanation, for example, but they may also need help understanding the divorce is not their fault. On the flipside, a teenager might adjust better to the changes ahead, but they may also want to hear more details and ask questions. Make sure your kids understand they can come to either of you if they are confused or upset about the divorce.

Remind them it's normal to feel emotional.

Your kids may not want to show you how they feel about the divorce, so make sure you communicate that their feelings are normal. Whether they are sad, angry, scared, or anxious, let them know these are natural reactions. Establish an open, ongoing dialogue with your children, so they feel comfortable discussing their thoughts and emotions with you. It also helps to reassure them that they are loved by both parents, regardless of the new living situation.

Avoid fighting in front of them.

If you genuinely want to shield your kids from the negativity of divorce, you should absolutely never fight in front of them. Studies show that children tend to adjust much worse to divorce when they are exposed to ongoing battles between parents. It may be difficult getting along with your ex-spouse, especially when conversations about finances or scheduling get heated, but there is no reason to let your kids overhear it. Make sure they are not around when you have these discussions. You should also try to cooperate with your ex as much as possible, even if you need a set conflict resolution plan to do it.

Avoid bad-mouthing your ex in front of them.

Although you will be living separately, your children still love both of their parents. Do not put them in a position where they have to choose loyalty to one or the other. That means avoiding the urge to assign blame or bad-mouth the other parent. If they feel stuck in the middle of your conflict, they may feel guilty and avoid speaking to you about their honest feelings.

How can I help my children cope with a bad-mouthing or manipulative parent?

My go-to resource on parental alienation issues is a book called *Divorce Poison* by Bart Warshak. One thing to understand is that you're not going to be able to deal with this with your own or directly with the other parent, at least in all likelihood. You need to make sure the parent has a good relationship with other family members or friends of the family, and you have a good support group for them.

You should definitely, if you think that's a problem, see about getting a family counselor involved.

After a stressful divorce process, it can be especially frustrating to realize your ex-spouse has been bad-mouthing you in front of your children. It's an awkward position to be in: do you let the comments slide in favor of keeping the peace, or fight back and risk trapping your kids in the middle?

When your ex is telling tales about you, you may naturally worry that the conflict will just end up alienating the children. What's more, if your ex is generally uncooperative, it may not be as simple as having a civil conversation with them and smoothing things out. Whatever the case, you may want to have a sit-down chat with your kids to alleviate any anxieties they might have about the conflict.

Look for the signs

Recognizing the red flags of a bad-mouthing parent is essential. Depending on the age and personality of your kids, it may be easy enough to recognize bad-mouthing when they simply repeat what your ex has said. In other cases, the signs are subtler. Your child might start to mimic your ex by absorbing attitudes or opinions that the other parent has about you. Children in these situations might also begin to reject the "target" parent or avoid contact with them, in which case you may want to investigate further.

Understand that kids exaggerate

If you're going to handle the situation appropriately, you should get your story straight—as well as your sources. Sometime kids may exaggerate or joke about a stressful situation without either parent being none the wiser about what was actually said or done. Before you confront your ex or take other steps, calmly ask your child for more details.

Watch your children's body language and facial expressions when you're listening to them as this can be a good indicator of the truth. Once you have a clearer picture, you'll be set to decide on your next move.

Don't fight fire with fire

You may be tempted to fire back at your ex with your own barrage of insults and accusations, but that's hardly the way to smooth things over with your kids. Resist the urge to raise your voice, respond with name-calling, or show anger toward the other parent. Instead, try to stay calm and respond from a place of empathy. Acknowledge that your child must have been hurt by the bad-mouthing, and gently correct the statement without getting defensive.

Don't brush it off

Retaliation is off-limits, but that doesn't mean you have to be a pushover. Ignoring or brushing off the other parent's comments could only lead to more confusion with your child. You're aiming for balance in this situation: you'll want to address your child's concerns, both without beating around the bush and without getting hot-tempered. It's a delicate balance to strike, but it gives your children more tools to cope with the situation.

Correct misinformation

Part of addressing your child's concerns involves calmly, gently correcting any misinformation or outright lies coming from your ex-spouse. Without implying, directly or indirectly, that the other parent is a liar, get to the root of the issue and make sure your kids understand the truth. For example, did your ex accuse you of taking their money? You can start by telling your kids that you wish their other parent hadn't blamed you, and then explain that divorce has an effect on both parents' finances. (In other words, fight fire with facts.) You don't need to get into the nitty-gritty, especially with younger kids, but make sure you set the record straight.

Offer reassurance

You might notice your child behaving oddly as a result of the bad-mouthing. Maybe they seem anxious or concerned —or maybe they've been behaving more or less as usual. Whatever the case, part of your response to your ex's bad-mouthing should be to reassure your kids that everything is alright. When your ex spreads false information or exaggerations about you, he or she is trying to undermine your relationship with your kids. They may need reminders that they are safe and loved.

Be approachable

If your kids are having trouble processing the divorce and its aftermath, they will want to feel that they can come to you with any concerns. That's especially true if your ex-spouse is exposing them to nasty comments about you. When you discuss the divorce and your ex, stay calm and non- confrontational. Answer any questions they might have, within reason. Keeping an open, positive attitude will help your kids approach you when things get difficult with the other parent.

Acknowledge your child's feelings

It can sometimes be difficult to remember that when an ex bad-mouths you, you're not the only one who is affected. Your kids absorb a lot about the divorce, and the resulting conflicts, that you may not notice. When the time comes to talk to your children about a badgering ex-spouse, make sure you take the time to understand their thoughts and feelings about the situation. It helps to verbally acknowledge how they must be feeling because it validates their emotions and makes you more approachable when they want to talk. This is also an aspect of teaching your kids to have agency over their own thoughts and feelings: they should understand that they can, and should, think for themselves.

Chapter 8

How do I decide not to be in the half of all marriages that end in divorce?

In Probability and Statistics 101, students learn how to use math to predict the chances of finding a blue marble after picking marbles randomly from a bag. This leads to countless engineering students who think people are marbles believing things like, "I shouldn't get married because half of all marriages end in divorce."

However, if some of those engineering students took a class from my sailing instructor, they would learn that every sailor has his own barrel of luck. By checking their safety equipment, following procedures, and so on, sailors can add good luck to their barrels. That way, when bad luck happens, there is a barrel full of good luck to draw from to get out of bad situations.

Bad luck: Man overboard!

Good luck: I practice man-overboard drills every month.

Lose your Divorce marbles.

We have a national barrel of two hundred million marriage marbles, one hundred million of which have "Divorce" written on them. That sounds daunting; however, those marbles aren't people. Instead, everyone gets his own bag of marbles. We can choose to throw out the whole bag, thereby eliminating the possibility of divorce, or we can choose to take some of the Divorce marbles out of our own bags.

For example, Billy Graham had a rule of not spending time alone with women to whom he was not married. Many people laugh this off as extreme or weak, but he decided to take fifteen Divorce marbles out of his bag. Not many people are willing to make that decision, and some deride it, but we should at least be honest about the choices we make.

An Estate Plan can help your marriage.

People think of Estate Plans, prenuptial agreements, and marital property agreements as planning for death and divorce. That creates an emotional barrier against doing something that can be very positive for your marriage.

<u>Walls are for prisons but also for playgrounds.</u>

Like building a wall around a playground, you can gain freedom by building walls around your separate and community assets. Streets create a zone of danger where children can't play. Putting up a wall transforms the danger zone into a play zone. Similarly, structuring your finances and marital property feels like you are walling yourselves in, but think of it as designing your own financial playground.

Too many people call my office with problems that could have been fixed by being intentional about their property and finances from the beginning instead of expecting things to just work out.

For example, Eddie liked to restore old cars. That was the tamest vice of any I had ever seen that lead to someone wanting a divorce, but Daphne wanted to retire someday. She was afraid that if she didn't divorce Eddie now, the damage caused by his expensive hobby would be so severe that her retirement plans could not be salvaged.

People lose their marbles when they are afraid.

Couples don't get divorced over money. Couples get divorced because their spouses are over-spending, they are scared about retirement, they are afraid that they will have to give up their dreams because their spouses are making the decisions, or they feel trapped because their spouses have complete control over all of the assets. The fear of losing independence, safety, and control leads to fighting, deception, and distrust. Fear causes them to behave badly and imagine things about each other to justify it. Eventually, someone reaches the end of the rope.

Daphne and Eddie's financial issues impacted their dreams. Dreams are a core part of who we are. With their cores threatened, they lashed out emotionally without thinking. Daphne and Eddie's arguments became increasingly severe and their words grew more vicious and cruel until their relationship became unsalvageable.

Their marriage should have started with an estate plan with marital property agreements, a financial plan, personal growth plans, and professional growth plans. If they had, there would have been walls around their assets so they could play without the fear of damaging the others' finances. They could have kept their dreams and been intentional about achieving them. A huge source of fear that leads to animosity and discord may never have materialized.

Don't put marbles in the espresso maker.

Like most marriages, I'm sure Daphne and Eddie's started with wedding gifts. They would have registered their wants and needs such as china, silverware, and kitchen appliances that would help them start their new life.

> **Bad luck:** Our dreams aren't as aligned as we thought!

> **Good luck:** We made financial plans before we married and update them every quarter.

Today, things are a bit different. Kitchenware isn't the big hurdle to marital bliss anymore. The world is now much more complicated — especially financially. Instead of giving newlyweds a cow and a milk jug, send them off with financial planning, estate planning, and career planning to give their new lives together a head start. You can take a lot more Divorce marbles out of their bags with the right estate and wealth plan than you could with an espresso machine.

Don't call people names.

It used to be quite the obvious rule, but it seems like it is broken everywhere these days. Why listen, acknowledge, and explain your position when you can just call people names and dismiss everything they say? Name-calling makes us stupider while making us feel smarter.

When May was in the hospital she would always send me pictures of bills. It didn't make much sense to me at the time. But then when I asked her to send me a picture of her room she got upset and start accusing me of not trusting her and trying to control her. I found the accusation offensive. Of course, when something like that happens, the first instinct is to think of the accuser in terms of an uncharitable colorful metaphor.

However, by not name-calling and labeling her, I was eventually able to work out the bigger picture and figure out that it wasn't about me. Fortunately, I had learned to acknowledge the colorful metaphors as they entered my mind and set them aside. Because May had been treated very badly in a previous relationship, she felt the need to prove where she was and how she was spending money. Since she was doing that by sending pictures of her bills, when I innocently asked for a picture of her room the existing connections in her brain told her that was an attack on her character.

I did not work out the big picture until much later, but I know from experience just how embarrassingly bad that fight would have been before I adopted the rule against name-calling. Instead, we were able to move past the misunderstanding and use all that energy to think about more important things.

Once you have become disciplined enough to stop your name-calling and dismiss other people's name-calling when they do it, your perceptions change dramatically. It is like unclogging drains all over your brain. Your mind is opened up to think more fully about the world you live in. You will become smarter and feel dumber, but it will improve your relationships.

These ideas won't remove all of the divorce marbles from your bag, but, based on my experience, they will help to remove a couple of handfuls.

Chapter 9

Final Thoughts

Love your enemy and the truth will set you free

In *Ender's Game* by Orson Scott Card, the protagonist, Andrew Wiggin, wins battles by loving the enemy. It sounds corny, but it is an insightful philosophy. Love, hate, and fear are reality-altering emotions. Love makes us search for truth and understanding. Hate and fear make us search for reasons to hate and fear more. Those reasons are almost always a misdirection which gives the enemy an advantage.

Years ago, I was loaded for bear preparing to cross-examine a witness who was helping to defraud my client. But then my client said the witness was a good person. I accepted that and very gently and carefully broke down her testimony with genuine concern for the position she was in. When the truth snuck out, a giant weight was lifted from her shoulders and she completely opened up. She wanted to be truthful, but she was trapped by a misguided loyalty to the wrong person. She would not have been nearly as helpful if I came at her antagonistically. A few months later I re-read *Ender's Game*, and my mind was blown. Orson Scott Card was right. If you want to win, love your enemy.

The road to Heck is paved with good intentions, and lawyers add a layer of grease to it.

Nowhere is this truer than in parental alienation cases. Here is a typical scenario.

Valerian and the Two Realities

April Alienator is paying child support to Valerian Victim. (It doesn't matter who pays. It works the same either way.) April is jealous of all the fun activities Valerian gets to do with the children with *her* money. She feels like she is being victimized and all her financial problems are Valerian's fault. She constantly frets about how she can't do anything fun with the children because Valerian is taking advantage of her by making her pay child support. Everything is unfair to her in her reality.

The children sympathize with April and want to help her. They start asking their father to be nicer to Mom and not take so much of her money. At first, Valerian tries to steer the children away from those types of conversations gently, but the children are persistent. They start getting into arguments, and their behavior deteriorates.

For months Valerian has been keeping his iguana under control and avoided talking bad about their mother. But now, fear of his children turning against him is taking over. His iguana starts fighting back and calling her names. What could be more evil than turning children against their father? Valerian's ever-worsening diatribes about their mother upset the children who don't understand why their father must be so mean about April.

Because the children come to visit upset with how Vincent talks about her, April limits the children's contact with the father over their long summer visitation. The children have no contact with Vince or any of his family, so they get no exposure to anything positive about them. Near the end of her visitation, April takes the children to a counselor that her attorney recommends. The counselor gets a one-sided history from the children, the attorney gets a restraining order, and a modification is initiated on short notice with the deck stacked heavily against Valerian.

Valerian *knows* that April doesn't really care about the children. She just wants child support. If she cared about the kids, she wouldn't have turned the children against him. They had a great relationship before she started causing problems.

Before you get stuck on what a lousy parent you think April is, you need to understand that both parents participated in training the children to be alienated. Because you see Valerian as the victim (possibly because I told you to), you don't understand April's reality and aren't asking what lead her down that path. That's important. Valerian chose a path too. He chose to hate the enemy, and it caused him to make bad decisions that trained his children to distrust his words.

Think about how you react if someone you love behaves incorrectly towards your children versus someone you love. The difference is huge.

It only takes one parent loving the enemy parent to help the children find truth and understanding, which is what children crave. Love for your children won't stop alienation but loving the alienating parent might help you prevent it.

Final thought.

Love your enemy. That doesn't mean you have to surrender, and it doesn't mean don't fight. You want to win, and if your primary goal is the best interest of your children, then I want you to win too. It says so in my contract.

Use love to think past the hate and fear. That way you can use your big brain to find the truth behind the shadows in the dark instead of letting fear and hate make your iguana see monsters. Even if it is a monster, you can't fight its shadow.

Good Luck!

Preston Park, J.D.
Law Office of Preston Park, PLLC
Plano, Texas

https://planocustodyhelp.com
Tel: 972-454-9743

Resources:

Adams, S. (2014). *How to fail at almost everything and still win big: Kind of the story of my life*. New York, NY: Portfolio/Penguin.

Carnegie, Dale, 1888-1955. (2009). *How to win friends and influence people*. New York :Simon & Schuster.

Dale Carnegie Course,
https://www.dalecarnegie.com/en/cours es/effective-communications

Warshak, R. A. (2002). *Divorce poison*. New York: HarperCollins World.

Welcome Back, Pluto
Understanding, Preventing, and Overcoming Parental Alienation™,
http://warshak.com/pluto

Collaborative Divorce Texas
https://collaborativedivorcetexas.com

Law Office of Preston Park, PLLC Blog,
https://planocustodyhelp.com/blog/

TexasLawHelp.org,
https://TexasLawHelp.org

Hill, N. (2019). *Think and grow rich.* Place
of publication not identified: ST
MARTINS *ESSENTIALS.*

Maxwell, J. C. (2014). *The 15 invaluable
laws of growth: Live them and reach your
potential.* New York: Center Street.

Card, O. S., & Harris, J. (2017). *Enders
game.* New York: Tor.

BIFF Response® Method, High Conflict
Institute,
https://www.highconflictinstitute.com/b
iff-responses

"The Gray Rock Method of Dealing
With A Narcissist When No Contact
Isn't An Option."

https://www.aconsciousrethink.com/6158/gray-rock-method-dealing-narcissist/

✔ Take action to find peace of mind

Thank you for choosing to read my perspective on how our iguana's can make family law cases more traumatic and expensive than they need to be. Hopefully, you have been able to find some nuggets of information that will take you down path that will lead to less stressful litigation, co-parenting, or whatever issues you may be facing.

Call our office at **972-454-9743** and mention this book for a free strategy session (a $300 value).

Sincerely,

Preston Park

Notes:

72719999R00061

Made in the USA
Columbia, SC
01 September 2019